A Walk with HOPE, Diabetes's Best Friend

Written and Illustrated

By Pamela Roller

AuthorHouse™
1663 Liberty Drive
Bloomington, IN 47403
www.authorhouse.com
Phone: 1 (833) 262-8899

Because of the dynamic nature of the Internet, any web addresses or links contained in this book may have changed
since publication and may no longer be valid. The views expressed in this work are solely those of the author and do not
necessarily reflect the views of the publisher, and the publisher hereby disclaims any responsibility for them.

Any people depicted in stock imagery provided by Getty Images are models,
and such images are being used for illustrative purposes only.
Certain stock imagery © Getty Images.

This book is printed on acid-free paper.

ISBN: 978-1-6655-0472-0 (sc)
ISBN: 978-1-6655-0473-7 (e)

Print information available on the last page.

Published by AuthorHouse 10/16/2020

authorHOUSE®

Dedication Page

This book is dedicated to every type of diabetic: Type 1, Type 2, gestational, and pre-diabetes, and to all of their families.

It is also dedicated to my late father, Glenn Burle Roller who had Type 1 Diabetes in his youth. I have great respect for what he went through over eighty years ago trying to manage diabetes without the latest technical devices.

Diabetes was curious to learn about itself so it decided to ask some animals what diabetes was. Diabetes asked, "Hippopotamus, what exactly is diabetes?"

"Diabetes is a disease that no one in the whole world wants. It attacks an organ in the body called the pancreas, and it is located behind the stomach. Diabetes destroys the cells that make insulin. Without insulin, blood sugar levels get dangerously high." answered Hippopotamus. "Oh, oh no, continued Hippopotamus, I'm about to sneeze! Ah Choo! For more information, why don't you ask the bees?"

Diabetes happened to see some bees busy pollinating. "Bees can you tell me 'please' something else I need to know about Diabetes?" It inquired.

"Fighting the disease is a twenty-four hours a day; seven days a week; three hundred and sixty-five days a year job. It is really frustrating, exhausting, expensive, and scary!" cried the Bees.

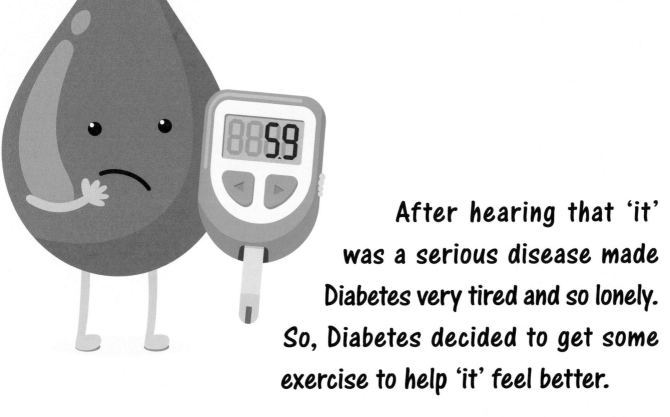

After hearing that 'it' was a serious disease made Diabetes very tired and so lonely. So, Diabetes decided to get some exercise to help 'it' feel better.

It could have done some jumping jacks or lots of push-ups, but that wouldn't help Diabetes make that many friends. After thinking about what Hippopotamus and the Bees said, Diabetes decided to go for a walk to find some friends.

First, Diabetes met an adorable brown puppy named HOPE. "I'm going for a walk to find some friends." "HOPE, would you be my friend?" asked Diabetes.

"Sure," yapped HOPE. "I will be your forever friend!"

Diabetes responded, "You're my only friend."

"Why don't we keep walking, and maybe we'll find some more friends!" said HOPE.

Along the way, they met a striped cat. "Cat, would you be my friend?" asked Diabetes.

Cat answered, "Oh dear, I have a fear of finger sticks and insulin injections; I want no part of that!"

Next, they met a hen. "Hen, would you be my friend?" questioned Diabetes.

Hen replied, "No, I have little chicks to feed and take care of, I don't want to take insulin!"

Then, Diabetes and HOPE met a green tortoise. "Tortoise, would you be my friend?" asked Diabetes.

"I may be slow, but I don't want my blood sugar to keep going really high and very low!" muttered Tortoise.

After that, they met a big black porcupine. "Porcupine, would you be my friend?" inquired Diabetes.

"No, no, no, my needles aren't for prickly finger sticks!" stammered Porcupine.

Diabetes and HOPE kept going. Then, they met a tall brown camel. "Camel, would you be my friend?" questioned Diabetes.

"No way, my humps aren't to be used for insulin pumps!" groaned Camel.

Finally, Diabetes and HOPE met a friendly little horse. "Horse, would you be my friend?" asked Diabetes.

"No, I don't want to count all of my carbs; I just like eating them of course!" neighed Horse.

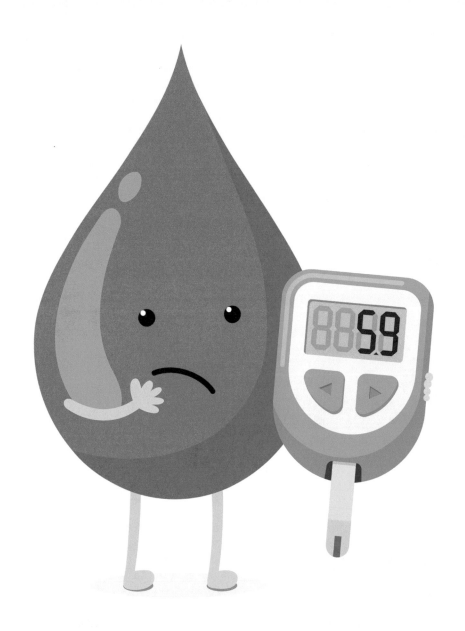

All of this made Diabetes very sad.

"HOPE, I just need to stop and rest!" sighed Diabetes.

After a long nap, Diabetes and HOPE continued on their walk to find some friends. They saw a big gray mole. "Mole, would you be my friend?" asked Diabetes.

"The only way I would be your friend is if Diabetes is under control!" shouted Mole.

Soon, they saw a lively brown owl near a big red barn.
"Owl, would you be my friend?" inquired Diabetes. "Oh me,
oh my, Diabetes is on the rise; you need lots of exercise, and
finding a cure would be wise!" insisted Owl.

Later, Diabetes and HOPE came to a pond and saw a little fish. "Fish, would you help me find a cure?" questioned Diabetes.

"Just never ever give up trying to find a cure is my wish!" stated Fish.

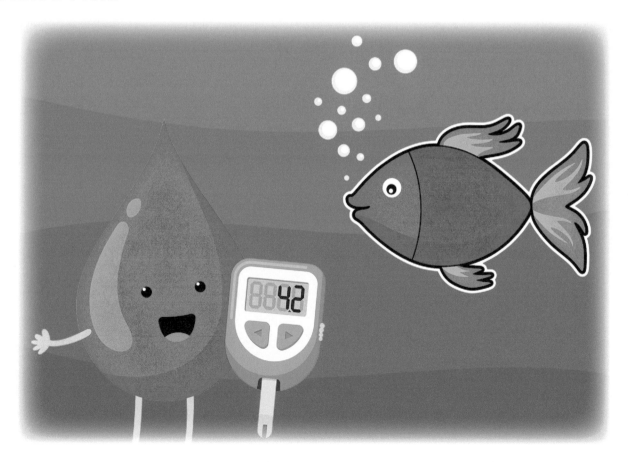

As they left the pond, they spotted a little bluebird on a tree branch. "Bird, would you help me find a cure?" asked Diabetes. "Sitting on this limb as my perch, I can tell you finding a cure takes lots of research!" declared Bird.

Nearby, they spied a frisky monkey hanging from a tree as happy as could be. "Monkey, would you help me find a cure?"

"Well!" "Getting plenty of exercise and eating healthy smaller portions is the key!" replied Monkey.

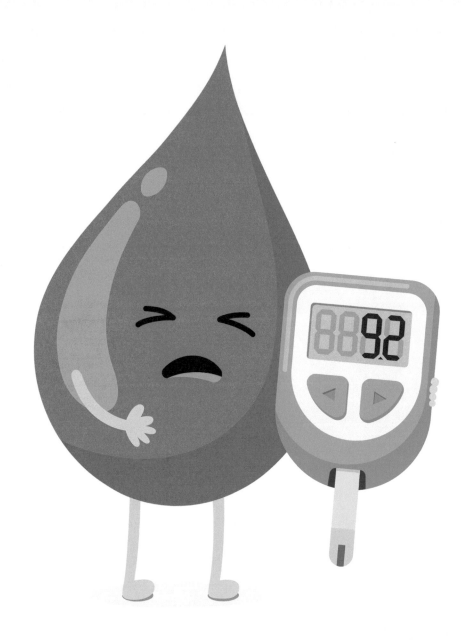

Diabetes screamed! "HELP!" "It is **TOO** hard fighting
Diabetes every day. No wonder nobody wants to be my friend!"

THEN, HOPE yelped. "I am your forever friend, 'Diabetes', and your only HOPE!"

"What do you mean by that?" cried Diabetes.

"WHY?" "My name spells it out BEST!" exclaimed HOPE.

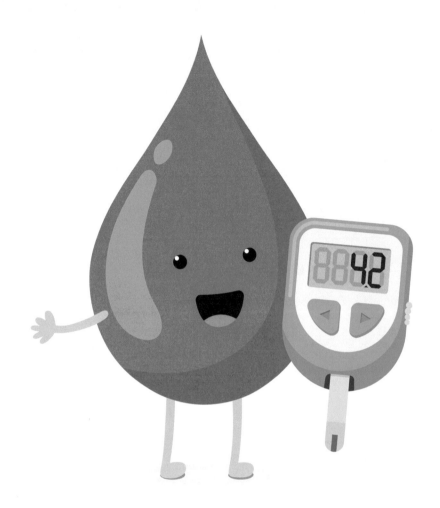

"**H** stands for being hopeful and always believing.

O stands for being optimistic and staying positive.

P stands for being persistent and never giving up.

E stands for having endurance to stay strong no matter what."

HOPE suddenly thought of a plan. She had a meeting with all of the animals 'Diabetes' met during their walk. HOPE and ALL of the animals gathered together and decided to help find the CURE.

"Until then,
Diabetes needs
our support!"
encouraged HOPE.

So, THEY. . .

Chose to help fight the disease

Unanimously and to be

Resilient and remain friends
until the

End of diabetes!

TOGETHER, they decided to
continue fighting for the
CURE!

ABOUT the AUTHOR

I was diagnosed with Type 1 Diabetes on October 24, 2018. This was something I didn't have on my radar! I had just retired after teaching 44 years, and I was about to enjoy the freedom to get to do the things I had always wanted to do.

After being diagnosed, I started a difficult journey that I could never have imagined. While fighting to live with diabetes and having been a lifelong educator, I felt led to make people more aware of this disease by telling my story and letting them know of its seriousness by encouraging them to watch for signs of its symptoms, and having screenings done regularly.

I organized the first annual World Diabetes Day event on November 14, 2019 in my hometown of Logansport, Indiana at a landmark called the Cass County Carousel. People of all ages enjoyed riding the historical carousel while trying to grab the BLUE ring. November is called a blue month for Diabetes Awareness.

I also created a Diabetes mascot called HOPE, Diabetes's Best Friend. She attended the event as well. HOPE was on hand to welcome everyone, especially the diabetics who ranged in ages from 3 to 95.

ABOUT Diabetes

World Diabetes Day is celebrated every year on November 14th. It is the birthday of Dr. Frederick Banting who discovered insulin in 1921 along with Dr. Charles Best.

The symbol for Diabetes is called "Unite for Diabetes". It is a blue circle. Blue represents the sky we all share worldwide, and the circle is for the unity it takes to fight for a cure.

Man's Best Friend and the Love of my Life

It was shocking to be told that I had Type 1 Diabetes. It meant learning how to give myself insulin injections. It has been a life changing experience. As a child, I was terrified watching my father give himself insulin shots daily prior to each meal. Seeing him go through diabetic reactions from extreme highs and lows was scary, and I had no clue what was going on. Towards, the end of his life, my father passed out while driving, hitting three parked cars, and causing his car to totally burn up. The good news was; he survived the crash.

Being diagnosed with Diabetes has been a life changing experience. Emotionally, I was a wreck so I asked my endocrinologist/diabetes doctor and my OB/GYN doctor to write letters of recommendation for an Emotional Support Animal. I started my first insulin injections October 25, 2018 and I received my Shih Tzu puppy on November 10, 2018. Patches was just weaned, and our journey together began. She gave me a reason to get out of bed each day, and she gave me the strength to fight this awful disease. While it takes a lot of work to take care of her, and to manage Diabetes, Patches has brought me great joy! She is a lot of company, very entertaining, and helps keep my blood pressure under control.

Before the pandemic hit with COVID 19, attending a local Diabetes Support Group was also very beneficial, and I also volunteered at Miller's Merry Manor in Logansport, IN. Once a month I held a Marvelous Monday event with theme related engaging activities and light refreshments for the residents. Patches came along with me, and the residents loved her. One Wednesday a month Patches also visited the residents. We called it Waggle-ly Wednesday. Both outings were something to look forward to, they gave me purpose as well as bringing joy to others. Patches just celebrated her second birthday by donating supplies needed at our local Humane Society.

Patches is the love of my life, and my fur-ever friend! I refuse to let Diabetes win! I will continue trying to make a difference in this world, despite fighting to live with the disease! Staying busy and focusing on making others happy has helped me cope! As long as I continue chasing my dreams and learning new things, I no longer feel like I am trapped in a Diabetes prison. It has made me a 'thrive to survive warrior' for a cure!

This book was written to promote Diabetes Awareness. Believe it or not, millions of people are battling Diabetes, and millions are walking around with Diabetes and don't know it. People don't believe it can happen to them; I didn't either. Please don't ignore the symptoms of this disease; get screened while there is still time!

Printed in the United States
By Bookmasters